To three of my biggest cheerleaders for PUG who passed away before they saw him in print - my beloved parents Ron and Lois James and Dr. Louis Traficante. A BIG heartfelt thank you to: my creative partners, Christine Barnes and Ron Mather; Exisle Publishing for introducing PUG to the world; all the people I love (you know who you are) for always being there for me.

First published 2017

Exisle Publishing Pty Ltd
PO Box 864, Chatswood, NSW 2057, Australia
226 High Street, Dunedin, 9016, New Zealand
www.exislepublishing.com

A CiP record for this book is available from the National Library of Australia.

ISBN 978 1 925335 62 0

Designed by Sarah Anderson
Typeset in Coustard
Printed in China

This book uses paper sourced under ISO 14001 guidelines from well-managed forests and other controlled sources.

10 9 8 7 6 5 4 3 2 1

PUG

PHILOSOPHICAL UNIVERSAL GUIDANCE

HOW TO BE THE

BEST YOU

Helen James

EXISLE PUBLISHING

We cannot be taught wisdom,
we have to discover it for ourselves
by a journey which no one can
undertake for us, an effort which
no one can spare us.

Marcel Proust. 1919

The world abounds with creatures
who can point the way.

PUG

MY NAME IS PUG. ALLOW ME TO INTRODUCE MYSELF.

I'm a Pug but no ordinary Pug.
I might look like a Pug, walk like a Pug and behave like a Pug,
but no other Pug looks at the world the way I look at the world.

My breed is one of the world's oldest.
And with age comes wisdom.
You could call me the world's first Pug Philosopher.
Who knows, maybe PUG stands for
Philosophical Universal Guidance.

For centuries Pugs have traveled the world
gathering experiences along the way.
My ancestors have been the favorite pets of Chinese emperors.
They've been companions to European royalty and
they have even lived with monks in Tibetan monasteries.

Pugs are loved by people all over the world.
So it's not surprising my view of the world is unique.
The time has come to share my thoughts with you in the hope
that you will find them inspirational and help you lead a
happier, more optimistic and fulfulling life.
I look forward to spending many moments with you.

THE JOURNEY

Think of your life as a journey,
one that will surely test you as
you seek to find yourself.
The slower you go, the more you will see.

CONFIDENCE

To explore new ground, you need
to have faith in yourself.
When following another, make sure
you pick the right leader.

SPIRIT

Before you can move forward, you
need to free your mind of the
thoughts that hold you back.

WONDER

When you look closely at what is
around you, an amazing world
comes into focus. It takes you
into the bigger picture.

AWARENESS

Focus on the present moment.
When you let go of thoughts about
things you cannot change or control,
everything becomes much quieter.

GRACE

Let your anger toward others float away.
Forgiveness sets you free.

RESILIENCE

In the midst of adversity, sometimes
only the sheer force of your will
can propel you forward.
Dig deep and you will find it.

RESOURCEFULNESS

When you find yourself in a
challenging situation, make it a
moment to set your imagination free.
Solutions will appear.

PERSEVERANCE

It is much easier to give up
when something seems too hard
to achieve. If your goal is
worthy, you will keep at it.

GRATITUDE

It's not always easy to maintain
a positive attitude. Try to focus
on the bright spots in your
life and be thankful for them.

JOY

Connecting with the lighter side
of life keeps you buoyant.
Laugh and play whenever you can,
even if only for a moment. It's contagious.

SING

Beautiful music and song
nourishes your whole being.
It lifts you up and, in the moment,
you fly away.

RELAXATION

Taking time out restores
vigor and clarity. It gets
you ready for the action to
begin again.

PERSPECTIVE

When you view your
circumstances in the context of
the bigger, wider world, it keeps
everything the right size.

HUMILITY

Those who remain humble are the
real winners in life. They understand that
no one is really better than anyone else.

LISTEN

Practice the art of paying attention.
When you are making all the noise,
you cannot hear anyone else.

BEAUTY

Beauty comes from the inside out.
When you avoid passing judgment
based on appearance, you will make
the unlikeliest of connections.

EMPATHY

If you imagine how the world
looks from the perspective of
another, you will have more
sympathy and understanding.

TOLERANCE

You can learn a lot from
others who are different from
you. Being respectful
leaves everyone at peace.

COMPOSURE

When you feel your hackles
rising, breathe deeply
and take a moment to cool off.

FRIENDSHIP

When you find a real friend,
be the friend you would like to
have. Sometimes it's just a matter
of knowing the other is there.

LOVE

When you are truly loved,
you feel safe, yet free to thrive.
Give your love back this way.

COMPASSION

Be alert to anyone who may
need help. Even a small
act of kindness can
lift the spirits of another.

COOPERATION

When you work with others to
achieve a common goal, it
leads to greater benefits for all.

GENEROSITY

The happiness you bring others
by sharing what you have
will inspire you to do it again.

REFLECTION

Take moments to pause and
ponder. You are the only one
who really knows who
your best self is.

PURPOSE

Taking the stance to be true to
yourself will unleash your power.
Use it to be a positive force
in the world.

BALANCE

When all the parts of
your being are in harmony,
you will find your poise.

TRANSFORMATION

Trying to be your best self is a choice
in any moment. Accept that you are a work
in progress and celebrate your journey
toward a better, happier self.

Remember, if you miss a moment,
take the next one.

I am not my past or what has
already happened to me.
I am what I choose to become.

Inspired by the words of
Carl Gustav Jung